LITTLE BOOK  IDEAS

D1464837

Published 2012 by Featherstone Education, Bloomsbury Publishing plc
50 Bedford Square, London, WC1B 3DP
www.acblack.com

ISBN 978-1-4081-4561-6

Text © Judith Harries
Illustrations © Emily Skinner
Cover photographs © Shutterstock

Printed in Great Britain by Latimer Trend & Company Limited

This book is produced using paper that is made from wood grown in
managed, sustainable forests. It is natural, renewable and recyclable.
The logging and manufacturing processes conform to the environmental
regulations of the country of origin.

210088
£12

**To see our full range of titles
visit www.acblack.com**

Contents

Introduction

The aim of this Little Book is to provide practitioners with ideas for developing young children's drama skills using links to well-known children's stories, popular picture books, traditional tales and stories from around the world.

Stories are used in the early years as a source of inspiration for learning across the whole curriculum. Picture books are easy for young children to relate to as many include familiar characters, events and experiences so that taking the next step into dramatising them is a very natural process.

Drama helps children to recognise problems and solutions within a story. They can develop their ideas and imagination alongside dramatic skills or techniques. Drama activities help to organise movements, thoughts, vocal control, inflections, gestures and body language. Children can be encouraged to make personal connections with stories. It's important that they have opportunities to present and share their work with others and receive constructive criticism.

Drama is an ideal vehicle for combining all areas of learning and the activities included in this book can be clearly used to help children make progress towards experiencing the prime areas of the newly proposed EYFS framework.

Links with the EYFS framework
Prime areas of learning and development

Personal, social and emotional development
▶ **Self-confidence and self-awareness**
Drama activities and games definitely require children to try out new activities and talk about which ones they enjoy. They need to be confident to speak in a group and talk about their ideas about characters and stories.

▶ **Managing feelings and behaviour**
Drama encourages children to talk about and demonstrate how they and others show feelings. Many of the activities require them to work as part of a group or class following agreed rules.

▶ **Making relationships**
This is not just about taking turns. However, many drama games develop this skill alongside encouraging children to respect and consider each others' ideas when they are involved in a dramatic activity or acting out a scene.

Physical development

▶ **Moving and handling**

Many of the activities include physical drama games that help children to show good control and co-ordination in large and small movements, and to move around confidently with spatial awareness.

Communication and language

▶ **Listening and attention**

Using stories requires children to listen attentively to books and storytelling, and to accurately interpret and anticipate key events. They will learn to respond to what they hear with relevant comments, questions and dramatic ideas and actions.

▶ **Understanding**

To get the most out of stories, children need to be able to follow layered instructions involving several ideas or actions and answer 'how' or 'why' questions related to characters, settings and actions.

▶ **Speaking**

Drama helps children to express themselves effectively and show an increasing awareness of an audience. The activities encourage them to develop their own narratives by connecting ideas to events in a story.

The specific areas of learning and development

Literacy
▶ **Reading** – Children are encouraged to read and recite simple sentences or lines from stories as they learn lines to dramatise them.

Understanding the World
▶ **The World** – The inclusion of traditional tales from different countries within the book will help children to see similarities and differences between countries of the World.

Expressive arts and design
▶ **Exploring and using media** – Many books lend themselves to creative ideas using a variety of arts and crafts materials, singing songs and making music.
▶ **Being imaginative** – Often the activities also suggest the creation of a role-play area to provide children with further opportunities to develop imaginative play.

How to use this book

Each session starts with a short resource list, including the book. There are suggested warm up games and then a variety of dramatic activities or 'strategies' linked to the story. There are often simple opportunities to talk about matters arising from the story – Chatterpoints. Story breaks are included as suggestions for how to break up the telling of the story to create more dramatic effect. Many other drama skills suitable for early years are covered such as Role on the wall, Freeze frames, Rolling theatre and Hot seat. Some stories also lend themselves to the creation of a Role-play area related to the story and there are details of how to set these up. Some sessions end with ideas for hands on Creative activities, including making props and masks which can then be used in the drama. All of these strategies are explained in more detail on pages 7-8.

The ideas in this book can be treated as complete drama sessions using each story as a stimulus for an hour of different experiences, culminating in a dramatic retelling of the story scene by scene or can be used as a resource from which to select one-off games or activities to fit in with the early year's balanced curriculum.

Here are some suggestions of useful organising strategies for drama sessions:

▶ Sit the children in a circle to play drama games and listen to stories.

▶ When moving on to the next activity try singing songs, particularly simple echo songs, using familiar tunes:

Find a space, find a space
In the room, in the room,
Can you find it quickly, can you find it quickly,
It's a race, it's a race.
(Tune: 'Frère Jacques')

We're going to work in twos, in twos,
Hoorah, hoorah.
(Tune: 'The ants go marching')

Hot seat,
Here's the hot seat.
(Tune: 'Flintstones')

▶ For partner work, invite children to work with their 'talk partners' selected
each week for use in all areas of the curriculum. Alternatively, let them choose
a friend who they work well with but keep an eye on any challenging pairs!
These pairs can then be asked to work with another pair or more to create
groups for Rolling theatre and other group activities.

Drama strategies

▶ **Warm ups**
Begin the 'journey into the story' by playing a game or activity that lets the
children become aware of concepts within the story.

▶ **Chatterpoints**
Key points in a story to talk or 'chat' about. Let children share their ideas and
impressions of characters, events and outcomes.

▶ **Story breaks**
Some stories work well if the children are left guessing what happens next!
Use story breaks to divide up the narrative into manageable chunks for
introducing drama activities and relevant games.

▶ **Tableau images**
Build up a picture from the story and create a still image or photograph/snap
shot of an event or scene. Sit or stand in a circle and add characters to the
scene one at a time.

▶ **Freeze frames**
Stop action to create a freeze frame.

▶ **Guided tour**
Lead the children around the room describing a setting. Point out any key
features that add to the story.

▶ **Thought tracking/tapping**
Share thoughts or feelings from a freeze frame. Tap a character on the
shoulder and ask them to share their thoughts. Just verbal or you can record
using thought or speech bubbles.

▶ **Hot seat**
A good way to get to know a character. Question different characters about
their feelings at various points in the story. It is often useful to use the

practitioner or teacher in role or a puppet as the character to be put in the hot seat.

▶ **Practitioner/Teacher in role**
You act and speak as though a character from the story. Using a simple prop or voice change can help children identify when you are in role. Alternatively, you can choose to use a puppet to act out the character.

▶ **Role on the wall**
Stick a picture of character on the wall. Let children choose words to describe the character, scribe them on post-it notes and stick to the picture.

▶ **Improvisation**
Spontaneous make-believe talk and actions that explore relationships, thoughts, behaviour and events. Improvisations can generate original material for role-play or performance.

▶ **Conscience alley**
Children stand in two lines facing each other. A child in character walks down the alley and the two lines speak out what they think is in the character's conscience.

▶ **Rolling theatre (scene by scene)**
Groups of children create parts of a scene and then run them in sequence to roll the whole scene or story. It's important that each mini-scene has a clear start and finish.

▶ **Physical drama**
Children are encouraged to use their bodies to practise different elements of the story often using exaggerated movements.

▶ **Partner work**
Working in pairs gives children more confidence to try out ideas with one other child before sharing with the whole group. More detailed skills and story events can be practised in this format.

Traditional stories

The Boy who Cried Wolf

An Aesop's fable (also called The shepherd's fable)

What you need:

▶ the book or story (www.aesops-fables.org.uk)

▶ a tambourine

▶ large pieces of paper, post-it notes and pens

▶ materials to make masks

Warm up:

Play this opposites game: Invite two children to challenge each other to say the opposite to any word you say. The quickest to answer is the champion and can challenge another child.

Try this 'Yes is No' game: Think of a simple question that requires a 'yes' or 'no' answer. Invite children to try and answer the question with the 'opposite' or wrong answer without laughing. For instance if you ask a boy, 'Are you a girl?' he should answer 'yes'.

▶ **Chatterpoint** – Is it right to give the wrong answers? Talk about how really important it is to be honest and tell the truth. Is it ever okay to tell a lie?

Story break – Read or tell the story up to where the boy tricks the villagers into thinking the wolf has come to eat his sheep for the second time.

▶ **Physical drama** – Invite children to stand in a space in the room. Ask them to move around the room weaving in and out of each other as you shake a tambourine. Shout 'up' or 'down' and children must stop and either stretch their arms up or crouch down. Shout out 'sheep' and the children need to copy whatever action you make or follow you around the room. Shout 'villagers' and the children need to gather in a group and look angry shaking their fists in the air. Shout 'Wolf!' and the children must stand still and snarl like a wolf.

▶ **What's the time Mr Wolf?** – Play this version of the traditional game. Mr Wolf stands with his back to the other children or 'sheep'. They all chant the question together 'What's the time Mr Wolf?' and he replies with a time of day such as '2 o'clock'. The sheep then move two steps towards the Wolf. If the Wolf replies 'dinnertime' he turns and chases the sheep away and anyone he catches takes a turn at being the new wolf.

▶ **Hot seat** – Invite a confident child or go in role yourself as the boy. Let children take turns to ask the boy why he lied to the villagers about the wolf (he was bored, liked to cause trouble, often told lies, etc). What did he think might happen next?

▶ **Freeze frames** – Act out the scenes when the boy cries 'Wolf!' and the villagers rush up the hillside to help only to find he has tricked them. Freeze the frame with the angry villagers surrounding the boy. Tap different children on the shoulder so they can share their feelings about the situation.

Story break – Read or tell the rest of the story when the wolf really does come and the boy cries 'Wolf!' for the third time.

▶ **Role on the wall** – Draw around one of the children and stick the picture on the wall. Let children take turns to choose words to describe the boy at different times in the story, scribe the words on post-it notes and stick to the picture. How do they think he felt when nobody came to help him?

▶ **Creative activities** – Make sheep and wolf masks for the children to wear. Use cotton wool or grey fun fur and paint.

The Lion and the Mouse

An Aesop's fable

What you need:

▶ the book or story (www.aesops-fables.org.uk)

▶ a toy lion or mouse

▶ finger puppets

Warm up:

Sit in a circle and pass a small toy lion or mouse around. This could be a finger puppet, soft toy or plastic animal. Help the children to chant these words as they play the game: Pass the toy around, pass the toy around. If the toy stops at you, try and make a sound. Explain that if they are holding the toy at the end of the chant they must make the appropriate sound – pretend to be either a big roaring lion or a little squeaking mouse.

▶ **Physical drama** – Take on the shapes of the two animals and contrast their different sizes. How could the children make themselves look as huge and fierce as a lion with its shaggy mane of hair? Now can they curl up small and make themselves as tiny as a mouse?

▶ **Chatterpoint** – Talk about what they would expect to happen if a big lion met a tiny mouse.

Story break – Read or share the beginning of the story where the mouse wakes up the sleeping lion. The mouse begs the lion to forgive him and promises to help the lion in the future!

▶ **Partner work** – Ask children to work in pairs taking turns to act out the characters of the lion and the mouse at the beginning of the story. The mouse can tickle the sleeping lion. How will the lion react to start with? Can the mouse persuade the lion not to hurt him?

▶ **Hot seat** – Go into role as the lion and let the children ask how the lion felt at this stage of the story. Repeat with the mouse character. Invite children to take turns acting in role or using a puppet.

▶ **Concentration games** – Play 'Sleeping lions'. Ask the children to lie still on the floor and pretend to be asleep. Choose one child to be the mouse and carefully go around the sleeping lions, tickling them gently using a soft toy or finger puppet. Can the children keep still and stay asleep? Whoever stays still the longest is the winner.

Story break – Read or share the second half of the story. The lion now needs the mouse's help to escape the hunter's net. The mouse manages to nibble and bite through the ropes and the lion is free. Are the children surprised by this ending?

▶ **Physical drama** – Ask two children to volunteer as the lion and the mouse. Explain to the other children that they are going to use their bodies to create a net to trap the lion. Ask them to make a circle around the lion, with their arms and legs outstretched, toes and fingers touching. The mouse runs in and out of the openings between the children. On your signal, the mouse taps one child's arms and legs which they close – making a hole in the net big enough for the lion to escape. Another two children now take the roles of the lion and the mouse.

▶ **Creative activities** – Make masks for the lion or mouse using simple cardboard outlines. Stick wool or curled strips of paper onto the lion's mask to create a mane. Use white pipe cleaners or art straws as whiskers for the mouse.

Three Billy Goat's Gruff

What you need:

▶ the book or story
▶ a drum
▶ a balance beam or bench

Warm up:

Sit in a circle and ask children to count '1, 2, 3' over and over again. Choose an action for 1 – stamp feet, and say '2, 3' out loud. Add an action for 3 – touch head, and still say '2' out loud. Finally add an action for 2. Invite children to work with a partner and make up new actions for the numbers.

▶ **Physical drama** – In a suitable space, invite children to walk around until you tap the drum when they must 'freeze' and stand completely still. Practise this a few times. Then shout out '1' – they must move around like the smallest goat, making their body as small as they can and taking tiny light steps. Tap the drum to make them freeze. Shout out '2' – children change to the middle-sized goat. How will their body shape and steps change? Tap the drum again. Finally shout out '3' – children change to the biggest goat with big heavy loud steps. Mix and match.

Story break – Tell the story up to where the first goat meets the troll and safely crosses the bridge to reach the field of delicious green grass and apple trees on the other side.

▶ **Five second trolls** – Display some pictures of scary trolls (from books or online) for children to come and look at. Then ask children to move around the room taking care not to bump into each other. On your signal they have five seconds to freeze into the shape of a big, ugly, scary troll. Who is the scariest? Look at faces, body shapes, sounds, etc.

Story break – Read on up to where the third goat sets off to cross the bridge. What do the children think will happen next?

▶ **Hot seat** – Go into role as the troll. Let children ask questions about where you come from, why you are living under the bridge, if you really want to eat the goats, etc. How does it feel to be a scary troll?

▶ **Changing voices** – Compare the voices of the three goats. Which goat will have the highest voice? Ask children to work in groups of three and change their voices to suit the three goats. As well as changing pitch can the children change the dynamics? Which goat will have the quietest voice?

▶ **Rolling theatre** – Choose a child to be the scary troll sitting near the bridge/balance beam. Let the groups of goats take turns at walking across the beam and escaping from the troll. Practise saying lines such as Troll: 'Who's that walking on my bridge?' and Goat 1: 'Don't eat me! Wait for my brother who's much fatter and tastier than me.' Remind children to use different pitched voices for each goat.

▶ **Conscience alley** – Form the children into two lines facing each other. Ask a child to walk in between the two lines as either the troll or one of the goats. The children can call out how they think the character is feeling as he waits or walks across the 'bridge'.

Story break – Read or tell the end of the story. Let children work in pairs to act out the final confrontation between the big billy goat and the troll.

▶ **Creative activities** – Make masks for the billy goat gruffs and/or troll. Experiment with hairy gloves and furry feet.

Build a bridge using large construction bricks or climbing equipment.

Cinderella

What you need:

- ▶ the book or story
- ▶ a selection of different shoes
- ▶ a 'magic wand' or musical instrument
- ▶ music and player

Warm up:

Sit in a circle and place a selection of different shoes in the middle. Try Wellington boots, ballet shoes, slippers, trainers, fancy high heels, flip flops, sandals, ski boots, flippers, etc. Invite children to choose a shoe and take on the character of someone who would wear them, e.g. pretend to be a gardener in his green Wellington boots or a dancer wearing ballet slippers.

Story break – Read or tell the story up to where Cinderella is left at home when her ugly sisters go to the ball.

▶ **Greetings your majesty** – Ask one child to sit on a special chair or 'throne' with their back to the rest of the group. The other children take turns to walk up, bow and say 'Greetings your majesty'. Can the queen or king identify the child without looking behind them? If correctly guessed, swap places.

▶ **What's my line?** – Cinderella has to do all the chores at her house. Make a list of what these jobs are – scrubbing, sweeping, laying the fire, ironing, washing clothes, dusting, peeling vegetables, cleaning windows, cooking, making beds, etc. Invite ideas from the children for how to mime some of these jobs. Sit in a circle and ask children to take turns miming a job for the others to guess.

Story break – Read the rest of the story all the way to the happy ever after ending.

▶ **Roles on the wall** – Put up a picture of the fairy godmother. Help children to scribe words to describe her. Repeat with other characters from the story such as the ugly sisters, Cinderella and the Prince.

▶ **Drama faces** – How does Cinderella feel at different points of the story? Ask children to show appropriate facial expressions for the beginning – Cinders working hard (tired); not able to go to the ball (sad); middle – the appearance of the fairy godmother (amazed); meeting the Prince at the ball (happy); returning to the house at midnight (in love!); end – the Prince comes round with the glass slipper (excited).

▶ **Transformations** – Talk about the changes that the fairy godmother's magic wand makes happen. Ask children to walk very slowly around as though dressed in rags, with hunched shoulders and sad faces, etc. Tap them with a magic wand or use a musical signal and let them instantly be transformed into fine clothes – with heads held high, walking more quickly or skipping and smiling. How could they act out the other transformations in the story – a pumpkin into a coach, mice into horses, or a lizard into a coachman!

▶ **Conscience alley** – Talk about the ugly sisters' roles in the story. Ask children to stand in two lines facing each other. Invite two children to walk down the 'conscience alley' in role as the ugly sisters, and ask the other children to speak out as their consciences.

▶ **The last waltz** – Ask children to find a partner and dance to some recorded waltz music as though at the ball. Dressing up is optional!

The Gingerbread Man

What you need:

- ▶ the book or story
- ▶ a gingerbread man puppet
- ▶ play dough scented with ground ginger and biscuit cutters

Warm up:

Stand in a circle and call out one of these statements: 'change places if you are wearing red/have black hair/like oranges/your name begins with M/like horses/like gingerbread, etc.' How quickly can the children find a new place to stand?

▶ **Lists** – Sit in a circle and invite children to take turns to name an animal. Make as long a list of names as possible. Try not to repeat any animals. Some of these animals can be added to the story.

Story break – Read or tell the story up to where the gingerbread man comes to the river.

▶ **Partner work 1** – Ask children to work with a partner. Take turns to be the gingerbread man and each of the animals he meets. Let children choose which animal they are going to be. Try using the words from the story for each animal', 'Stop, I want to eat you.' The gingerbread man has to say 'Run, run as fast as you can. You can't catch me, I'm the gingerbread man!'

▶ **Choral speaking** – The repeated words of the gingerbread man (see above) are great for practising speaking and listening. Invite all the children to try reciting the words together.

▶ **Physical drama** – Ask the children to find a space in the room. Explain that they are going to be the gingerbread man running away from the old couple and all the animals towards the river. Remind them to take care to avoid bumping into anybody. Change the action every 15 seconds – run, hop, skip, jump, slide, creep, etc. Try some more dramatic actions, e.g. walk backwards, roll, crawl, hobble, march, scramble, race, stroll, strut, limp, etc.

▶ **Follow my leader** – Choose a child to be the gingerbread man and lead the old couple and all the animals around the room. The children must copy all the different ways that the gingerbread man moves. When you shout 'River!', all of the children must stop.

Story break – Read the next part of the story when the fox offers to help the gingerbread man across the river. What do the children think will happen to him? Read to the end and see if they guessed correctly.

▶ **Hot seat** – Go into role as one of the key characters the (old woman, gingerbread man, fox) or use a puppet. Encourage the children to ask questions of each character. How did they feel at different parts of the story?

▶ **Partner work 2** – Ask the children to work with their partner in the characters of the gingerbread man and the fox and act out the end of the story as the fated biscuit jumps from the fox's tail, to his back, to his neck and finally onto his nose!

▶ **Role-play** – Set up a kitchen in the role-play area. Provide lots of cooking utensils, scales, packets, cutters, rolling pins and ginger-flavoured play dough. Let the children dress up in aprons and chefs hat as they make their gingerbread man 'biscuits'.

▶ **Creative activities** – Make some real gingerbread man biscuits.

Rumpelstiltskin

What you need:

► the book or story
► painting materials
► spinning or 'angry' music and CD player, musical instruments

I will need

Warm up:

Play 'New names': Invite children to make up alliterative names for themselves by thinking of a describing word that starts with their initial letter, such as Sad Sally, Gentle Georgina, Jumping Johnny, Talking Tali, etc.

Story break – Read or tell the beginning of the story when the miller goes before the king and boasts about his daughter.

► **An audience with the king** – Go into role as the king. Invite the children to take turns to come and 'boast' to the king about an extraordinary talent they have. They could pretend to be able to play an instrument, run very fast, or more crazy ideas such as fly like a bird, turn paper into sausages, etc.

▶ **Physical drama** – Ask children to stand in a space and to imagine that they are a piece of straw – a long, thin, flexible, spiky stick. Play some spinning music, e.g. 'The Flight of the Bumble Bee' by Rimsky-Korsakov or Mendelssohn's 'Spinning song' and invite the children to spin round and around. On a signal, can they make the shape of a solid nugget of gold – cold, immoveable, small, etc.

▶ **Role on the wall** – Let children paint portraits of what they think the little man might look like. Choose one of their pictures to put on the wall. Help children to scribe words to describe the little man onto post-it notes and stick onto the picture.

▶ **Guessing name game** – Sit in a circle and take turns to guess names for the little man. Use names from the story and the children's own ideas for names. Encourage the children to be as imaginative as possible using real names and made up ones.

▶ **Partner work** – Ask children to find a partner. Take turns to take the roles of the queen and the little man in the scene when she is trying to guess his name.

▶ **Confrontation** – Go into role as the little man and invite children to take turns choosing three names. Get more and more excited as the names are wrong. Let the last child be the one who is allowed to guess correctly. How will Rumpelstiltskin react?

▶ **Rumpelstiltskin's dances** – Replay the spinning music and let the children do a crazy dance as Rumpelstiltskin sings his name song around the fire in his little house. Try chanting these words:

As I dance, as I preen,
I will win the child of the queen.
She won't guess, she won't win,
For my name is Rumpelstiltskin.

Listen to some angry music such as Bartok's 'Allegro Barbaro' or 'Rage over a lost penny' by Beethoven. Ask the children to invent a furious, angry dance in the character of Rumpelstiltskin at the end of the story.

▶ **Creative activities** – Make your own angry music using drums, tambours, tambourines and claves.

The Three Little Pigs

What you need:

▶ the book or story
▶ plastic drinking straws, pencils, Duplo or wooden bricks

Warm up:

Play 'Pass the shakes': Act surprised and begin to shake one part of your body such as your left hand. Explain that you have caught the 'shakes' and the only way to get rid of them is to pass them on! Choose a child in the circle, say their name and throw the shakes to them. They must then shake a different part of the body such as their right leg, and so on.

Story break – Introduce the story of the Three Little Pigs. Explain that at the beginning Mother Pig tells her three little pigs that they are grown up and have to move out. How will the little pigs react?

▶ **Three little pigs** – Ask children to work in groups of three and number themselves 1-3. Call out '1', and all the first little pigs must leave the group and shuffle and shake around the room. On '2', the second little pigs can move around with only one part of their body shaking, and on '3', the third little pigs can trot confidently around, looking brave! Swap round the numbers and repeat the game.

Story break – Continue the story up to where the first little pig has built his house out of straw. Can the children remember what happens next?

▶ **House building sound effects** – Divide the children into three groups. Give the first group pairs of straws and ask them to tap them gently together and whisper quietly 'straw straw'. Let the second group use pencils tapped together as they say a little bit louder 'sticks sticks'. Ask the third group to chant loudly – 'bricks bricks' as they tap wooden bricks together.

Story break – Read on to the end of the story.

▶ **Hot seat** – Go into role as the wolf and let the children ask him questions. How did he feel at different points of the story? Let him give his version of the story!

▶ **Physical drama** – Choose one child to be the first little pig and one child to be the wolf. Help the first little pig to arrange or 'build' the other children into a house made of straw. Ask five or six children to stand up in a circle with their arms streched up. Can they touch each other's fingers to create a roof? Ask the children to freeze frame the house shape that they have made. Then ask the wolf to approach the house and use the words from the story in appropriate voices:

Wolf: 'Little pig, little pig, let me come in!'
1st Little Pig: 'Not by the hair on my chinny chin chin, I will not let you in'.
Wolf: 'Then I will huff, and I'll puff, and I'll blow your house down!'

As the wolf huffs and puffs, instruct the children to start to shake and wobble and eventually fall over. Now repeat with the second little pig and his house of sticks. How will the children make this house seem stronger? Finally create the third little pig's house made of bricks. This time the house needs to shake a bit but not fall down despite the wolf's efforts! The three little pigs can gather in the house and decide on an ending. Will the wolf fall down the chimney or escape for another day?

The Town Mouse and the Country Mouse

An Aesop's fable

What you need:

- ▶ the book or story
- ▶ mice finger or hand puppets
- ▶ circles of white card
- ▶ a tambourine
- ▶ large pieces of paper

Warm up:

Make a collection of items associated with the countryside – a leaf, a stick, a flower, a toy cow, grass, and so on. Place them on a tray and ask children to memorise what is there. Then cover the tray and remove one item. Who can tell you what is missing? Repeat with items you could associate with the town e.g. a coin, small world play buildings, toy car, bus ticket etc.

Story break – Introduce the story and the two main characters using finger or hand puppets. Read or tell up to where the town mouse invites his cousin, the country mouse, to visit him.

▶ **Virtual tour** – Display pictures on an IWB of a typical country scene and a busy town or city scene as a backdrop to the story. You might use illustrations from the book or photos. Explain to the children that you are going to take them on a tour of each of the mice's surroundings and homes. Go into role as the country mouse and point out features of the country scene such as fields, farms, trees, hillside, birds, etc. Invite children to take turns to do the same. Repeat as the town mouse showing the children the tall buildings, shops and busy roads of the town.

▶ **Follow my leader home** – Invite a child to be either the town or country mouse leading the other children around their environment. Can they vary the things they see and places they go to suit the two different scenes. Set up a corner in the room labelled 'home' where the expedition ends. How do the children feel when they are safely home?

▶ **Chatterpoint** – Is it better to live in the country or the town? Encourage children to empathise with each other's feelings.

▶ **Physical drama** – Talk about how the two mice although being good friends behaved differently because of where they lived. Country mouse moves more slowly and takes things easy. Town mouse is the opposite and moves very fast and is rather proud. Ask children to show this contrast with their bodies. Use musical signals – fast shaking of a tambourine for the town mouse, head held high, busy scurrying everywhere, not caring about how much noise he makes and slow tapping on the tambourine as the country mouse plods around, creeping quietly or lazes in the sunshine.

Story break – Read to the end of the story when the country mouse rushes back to the safety of his home.

▶ **Hot seat** – Go into role as one of the mice. Can the children ask you 'yes' and 'no' questions to find out which mouse you are?

▶ **Partner work** – Ask children to work with a partner. Provide a large piece of paper and let them draw their own mini-backdrop either of the country or town. Brainstorm which things will be found in the different settings. Act out their chosen scene using finger puppets (see below).

▶ **Creative activities** – Make finger mice puppets using a semi circle of white card folded and fastened into a cone shape. Let children decorate their mice with appropriate colours or clothes for the country or town mouse.

Picture books

Angelina Sprocket's Pockets

by Quentin Blake

What you need:

- the book
- a large jacket or coat
- a small fabric bag
- different small objects (to hide in pockets)
- an old washing up bowl full of pans, forks, spoons, graters and buckets

Warm up:

Place a few small familiar objects such as an apple, a book or a small toy in a small fabric bag. Sit in a circle and pass the bag around the ring. Ask children to feel for an object in the bag and try to guess what it is without looking. Can they guess and then pull the item out of the bag to see if they're correct?

Story break – Introduce the character of Angelina Sprocket and read the complete story.

▶ **Memory game** – Go round the circle and invite each child to remember one thing that Angelina Sprocket has hidden in her many pockets. Use this phrase 'There's a pocket for ......' and see if they can create a complete list. Check back with the book to see if they have remembered everything.

▶ **What's in my pocket?** – Go into role as Angelina Sprocket. Pretend to take something from the story out of a pocket and mime using it such as a hanky, umbrella, swimming costume, motorhorn, or skateboard! Invite children to guess which item you are miming.

▶ **Physical drama** – Ask children to find a space in the room. Shout out different things from Angelina's pockets and ask children to mime using them. Encourage them to play 'What's in my pocket?' (see above).

▶ **Pocket dreams** – Invite the children to share their 'pocket dreams' and choose what they would most like to find in a magic pocket and why.

▶ **Role on the wall** – Copy and enlarge a picture of Angelina Sprocket from the book. Stick it on the wall and let children take turns to scribe words on notes to describe her character.

▶ **Angelina's coat** – Provide an over-sized coat for children to dress up as Angelina. Sew or pin on extra pockets using squares of fabric. Make a selection of small objects for children to hide in the pockets. Ask them to play a guessing game, describing the hidden objects for other children to identify.

▶ **Still image** – Make a still image from the story. Give out pans, buckets, forks and spoons, graters, and the kitchen sink.

▶ **Creative activities** – Make some Angelina Sprocket music. Use all the metal implements from 'Still image' to create some metal sounds. Suspend the items from a frame and tap with a triangle beater. Record and listen back.

Help children to make a pocket and sew or pin it onto their clothes. Have fun pretending to be Angelina Sprocket.

Dinosaurs Galore

by Giles Andreae

What you need:

- the book
- a small stage mat or carpet square
- dancing music

Warm up:

Sit in a circle and experiment with dinosaur sounds. Pass a 'roar' around the ring. Try starting quiet and growing louder and then quieter again as the dinosaur moves away.

▶ **Projections** – Invite children to stand at one end of the room while you stand at the other. Take turns to share any news – not shouting but projecting their voice across the room so they can be heard.

▶ **Stage mat** – This is a good opportunity for children to try learning words off by heart. The individual dinosaur rhymes are mostly four lines long and written in rhyming verse which makes them easier to learn. Let children choose a dinosaur verse to learn. Encourage them to present the rhyme standing on a special stage mat. Think about how to start the rhyme by introducing the title and the author. Talk about using a loud voice and projecting the words to the back of the room. Try to avoid shouting. Can they think of actions to go with their performance?

▶ **Dinosaur moves** – Check out Planet Dinosaur on BBC online and watch how different dinosaurs move. Explain to children that when you shout out each dinosaur name they should try to move in suitable ways. Start with the Diplodocus who plods slowly around taking huge dinosaur steps. Then introduce the Velociraptor who runs very quickly and has giant pointy claws. When the children are used to the contrast between these two, try adding the Tyrannosaurus Rex who moves in giant steps on two feet with two finger claws on his arms, the Stegosaurus who is on all fours and the Pteranodon who flies around with huge wings outstretched.

▶ **Musical dinosaurs** – Choose some suitable dancing music and invite the children to create a dinosaur dance. Each time the music stops can they freeze in the shape of their favourite dinosaur?

▶ **Let's meet the dinosaurs** – Present or recite the verses of the book one after the other like a dinosaur parade. Go into role as a dinosaur expert in a museum or a palaeontologist and introduce each one.

▶ **We're all going on a dinosaur hunt** – Use the well-known rhyme about going on a bear hunt and adapt it to hunt dinosaurs!

▶ **Role-play** – Set up a dinosaur dig in the role-play area. Separate the area with a string fence or stripy tape and then sprinkle sand onto the floor mats. Alternatively use the sand tray. Provide plastic hard hats, spades, buckets, tools, a variety of pebbles, rocks, plastic bones, big magnifying glasses, notebooks, etc.

▶ **Creative activities** – Make dinosaur fossils using play dough or clay and dry pasta.

Print dinosaur trails using the feet of plastic dinosaurs and paint. Lay the trails around the room for children to follow.

Farmer Duck

by Martin Waddell

What you need:

- ▶ the book
- ▶ a duck puppet or soft toy
- ▶ tools

Warm up:

Sit in a circle and invite children to practise making different animal sounds.
Then take turns to pass an animal sound around the circle with each child
making a different sound and see if the others can recognise which animal it is.
Try not to have any repeats!

▶ **Puppet in role** – Introduce the duck puppet to the children and try to make him look sad and tired. Can the children guess how he is feeling? Let the duck talk to the children by whispering to you. Make him tell them about all the work he has to do on the farm.

Story break – Read the story up to the point where poor Duck is too tired to go on anymore.

▶ **What's my line?** – Invite children to take turns to mime the different jobs on the farm for the group to guess. After each mime take time to improve the mime (choosing simple actions) and let everyone have a go.

▶ **Rolling dialogue** – Choose a child to be the farmer lazing in his bed. Help them to say the line 'How goes the work?' in a suitable lazy voice. Invite some of the other children to act out the Duck working hard and replying 'QUACK' each time. Follow the sequence of jobs from the book and create a rolling dialogue.

▶ **Meeting drama** – In role as one of the animals, call a meeting to talk about what is happening on the farm. Is it fair that Duck does all the work? What do the other animals think they could do to solve the problem? Consider their ideas carefully and make a plan!

▶ **Concentration game** – Ask one child to pretend to be the lazy farmer and face the wall. All the other children have to start at the other side of the room and creep slowly and quietly towards him. If he hears anything he must wake up, turn around and see if he can see somebody moving, then send them back to the start. The children must try and get close enough to touch him. Whoever succeeds can have the next turn at being the farmer.

Story break – Read to the end of the story and discover how the animals work together to get rid of the farmer.

▶ **Animal rescue** – Ask the children to choose to be either a cow, sheep or hen. Practise different ways of moving like the animals. As a group, mime creeping through the back door, into the house, down the hall, up the stairs, into the bedroom, under the bed, etc. Then use their animal sounds as they chase the farmer out of the bed, down the lane, through the fields, over the hill, etc.

▶ **Freeze frame** – Ask all the children to mime working at the different jobs together with the Duck and create a freeze frame to show the 'happy ending' of the story.

▶ **Role-play** – Set up a farmyard in the role-play area. Provide spades, brooms, and buckets for the children to use as they work on the farm. Dress up in Wellington boots and overalls. Use sit-and-ride toys as tractors and add soft toy animals or masks for the children to wear.

Lost and Found

by Oliver Jeffers

What you need:

▶ the book
▶ a soft toy penguin or puppet
▶ an umbrella
▶ blue fabric or elastic rope
▶ a suitcase
▶ sad music and a player

Warm up:

Pretend that there is a knock on the door. Let children take turns to say who they think is at the door. Ask them to pretend to open the door and see who is there. How will they react? Introduce the penguin toy or puppet at the door, looking sad. Why do the children think the penguin is sad?

Story break – Read the opening of the story.

▶ **Chatterpoint** – Talk about feeling sad. Pass the penguin toy around the circle and invite children to share what makes them feel sad. If they do not want to share ask them to pass the toy on.

Story break – Read about how the boy helps the penguin to find his home.

▶ **Packing game** – Sit in a circle and invite children to take turns sharing what the boy and the penguin will need to pack in their suitcase for their trip to the South Pole. Try this as an accumulative game starting with the phrase 'We will need to pack... a torch, some food, warm clothes, an umbrella, etc'. Let children mime finding each item, folding and packing it into the suitcase.

▶ **Physical drama** – Make a loop of elastic rope and sit the children in a circle holding onto the rope and pulling it out and in as though rowing a boat. Let them sing this song to the tune of 'Row, row, row the boat' as they move.

Row, row, row the boat
Row the boat to sea,
Rowing to the South Pole
Penguin and me.

As the storm breaks, the waves get bigger and the sea rougher. Make the rope move faster and exaggerate the rowing movements. Then as the storm subsides the rowing becomes calmer again.

▶ **Guided tour** – Use a picture on the IWB of the frozen South Pole environment. Lead the children around the room describing the setting. Point out any key features to create an atmosphere. Let the children hold their arms down by their sides like flippers and shuffle with their feet together so they can follow you around like penguins.

▶ **Thought tapping** – Ask children to imagine how the boy and the penguin are feeling when they reach the South Pole.

▶ **Feeling lonely** – Ask children to find a space in the room. Put on some sad music such as Barber's 'Adagio for strings', Bloch's 'Schelomo', or 'Tears in Heaven' by Eric Clapton. Invite children to weave in and out of each other slowly and silently. Can they try and look sad or lonely using their face and body and by avoiding eye contact with each other. When the music stops invite them to greet the nearest person and change their mood to a happy one.

Story break – Read the end of the story where the boy and the penguin are reunited.

▶ **Spot the penguin** – Ask for a volunteer (the finder) to leave the room while another child hides the penguin toy. Then the finder must try and find the toy and the rest of the group can use 'hot or cold' signals to help. How will the finder react when he finds the penguin? Place the penguin toy in an upside down umbrella.

▶ **Creative activities** – Let the children use a variety of musical instruments to create their own sad music.
Make paper penguins out of black and white sugar paper.

Olivia

by Ian Falconer

What you need:

- ▶ the book
- ▶ a soft toy pig or puppet
- ▶ brown paper bags

Warm up:

Stand in a circle and play a game of 'Change places'. Call out a fact such as 'Everyone wearing red' and all the children this applies to must change places. Think of different facts to help the children get to know each other 'Everyone who likes sausages/music/chocolate/carrots/drama/football, etc'.

Story break – Read the beginning of the story and introduce Olivia. You could use a small soft toy pig or puppet. Explain that she is good at lots of things.

▶ **Speaking and listening** – Sit children in a circle and invite them to take turns introducing themselves saying 'My name is...' and then adding 'and I am good at ...' Encourage them to speak loud and clearly so that everyone in the circle can hear them. Make suggestions for less confident children such as 'being a good friend' or 'being helpful'.

▶ **Wear yourself out** – Play a copying game in the style of 'Simon says' but use 'Olivia says' instead. Use some of the actions from the illustrations in the book.

▶ **Partner work 1** – Olivia's little brother Oliver is always copying. Ask children to work with a partner and take turns at being Olivia getting dressed in the mirror. The partner is Oliver and must try and copy every move she makes! Ask them to put on a vest, hat, dress, tights, tie a bow in their hair and even put on lipstick!

▶ **Partner work 2** – Look at the sandcastles Olivia builds. Play the 'sculptors' game. Working with a partner take turns to be the sculptor or the sand. Let the sculptor shape their partner into a statue, castle or building. Go round in role as a judge and see who has created the best model.

▶ **A day in the life of ...** – Read through the sequence of Olivia's day in the story. Help children to mime the sequence – gets up, moves the cat, brushes teeth, combs ears, moves the cat, gets dressed, goes to the beach, builds sandcastles, visits the museum, does some painting, time to think, has a bath, eats dinner, goes to bed (with 5 bedtime stories!), etc. Then invite children to create their own sequence of events for a typical day in their life and show them to the rest of the group. Can everyone guess what the children are miming? Sing this song to the tune of 'Here we go round the mulberry bush' and change the actions each time:

This is the way we get out of bed,
Get out of bed, get out of bed,
This is the way we get out of bed,
In a day in my life.

▶ **Dreams** – Encourage the children to think about what they would like to be when they are grown up. Can they do a simple mime to illustrate this? Turn this into a version of 'What's my line?' called 'What's my dream?'.

Story break – Read to the end of the story.

▶ **Creative activities** – Make a scary paper bag face for Olivia to use when she is tired of Oliver copying her! Use big brown paper bags and help children to cut out eyes and draw on scary teeth!

Do some Olivia dancing and painting!

Patrick

by Quentin Blake

What you need:

▶ the book
▶ a violin and some recorded violin music
▶ small hand mirrors

I will need

Warm up:

Show the children a violin. Pass it carefully round the group and let children handle it, pluck the strings, feel the shiny wood, and talk about what they can see. Listen to some violin music. Try happy Irish jigs and reels or Brahms 'Hungarian Dances' or sad music such as the theme from 'Schindler's List'.

▶ **Chatterpoint** – Does music make the children feel happy or sad?

Story break – Read the story up to where Patrick buys the violin from Mr Onion's market stall. What do the children think he will do with the violin?

▶ **Feeling faces** – Sit in a circle and show children a wooden spoon with a smiley, happy face on one side and a sad face on the other. Pass the spoon round and invite children to share what makes them feel happy or sad. Can they show how they feel by their facial expressions? Use small mirrors for children to look in and explore how happy or sad they can make themselves look.

> **Story break** – Continue reading the story and discover how the music Patrick plays on his violin transforms everything into technicolour!

▶ **Physical drama** – Remind the children of how their facial expressions change between happy and sad. Can they show this change with their body language? How will they move when happy – head held high, swinging arms, walking quickly or skipping, animated, etc. On a signal, can they change their bodies to show sadness – hanging head, moving slowly, hugging arms around body, shrinking, etc. Talk about how the fish, children, trees and cows are transformed by the music. How could the children demonstrate this change with their bodies?

▶ **Group drama** – Group children into fish, children, trees, birds, cows, the tramp, the tinker and his wife, etc. and go into role as Patrick. Let each group work on a transformation with their body shapes and facial expressions as Patrick comes along with his violin. Encourage children to offer their own ideas and try to work with them. Watch groups and talk about what works and what doesn't.

▶ **Follow my leader** – Use ideas from 'Group drama' to create a colourful procession. Let children go into role as Patrick and take turns leading the children around the space. Sing this song to the tune of 'Aiken Drum' as you go:

There was a man called Patrick,
Patrick, Patrick,
There was a man called Patrick
And he played the violin.

He played magic music,
Music, music,
He played magic music,
On his violin.

▶ **Chatterpoint** – What things or people would the children choose to change with Patrick's magic music?

▶ **Hot seat** – Choose different characters such as Kath, Mick, the tramp, the tinker and his wife to go on the hot seat. Let the other children ask them how it felt when they heard the music. How did they change for the better?

▶ **Creative activities** – Provide lots of paints and ask children to create before and after portraits for the different characters and animals in the story.

Peace at Last

by Jill Murphy

What you need:

- ▶ the book
- ▶ a variety of musical instruments
- ▶ materials to make bear masks

Warm up:

Children sit in a circle with one child in the middle who pretends to be Mr Bear, fast asleep. Place a musical instrument next to him or her. Invite another child to creep up to the sleeping bear and steal the instrument shaking it as they go. Then she/he sits back in the circle and places the instrument behind her/him. All the children then shout 'Wake up Mr Bear!' Mr Bear wakes up, stretches and yawns and tries to guess who is hiding his musical instrument.

► **Chatterpoint** – Talk about feeling tired. Let the children pretend to be tired. How will they show this? Try doing things as though tired – walking, eating, talking, playing, etc. Why is it important to get enough sleep?

Story break – Read the opening of the story when all the Bear family are very tired.

► **Sound effects story** – Make a list of the sounds that keep Mr Bear awake. Let children experiment with different musical instruments and voices to create sound effects for the various sounds – Mrs Bear snoring, Baby Bear pretending to be an aeroplane, clock ticking, dripping tap, humming fridge, owl hooting, hedgehogs and cats in the garden, and birds singing.

► **Teacher in role** – Go into role as Mr Bear (wearing pyjamas and/or dressing gown) and talk to the children about how he felt when he was trying to get to sleep. Can the children think of anything Mr Bear could do to help him go to sleep?

Story break – Read the rest of the story to the children.

► **Rolling theatre** – Divide the story into scenes – Mr and Mrs Bear's room, Baby Bear's room, living room, kitchen, garden, car. Using different Mr Bears and suitable sound effects combine the scenes into a rolling theatre of the story. At the end of each scene all the children can help Mr Bear say 'Oh NO! I can't stand THIS'.

► **Role-play** – Set up the home corner as Mr Bear's house with the different rooms in the story. Provide pyjamas, dressing gowns and slippers for the children to dress up in and lots of chairs, beds, bedding and pillows for Mr Bear to use. Place the musical instruments that the children used for sound effects in the rooms so they can act out the story independently.

► **Creative activities** – Make bear masks using a simple template covered in brown paint, wool, felt and other furry materials.

Six Dinner Sid

by Inga Moore

What you need:

- ▶ the book
- ▶ a soft toy or puppet cat
- ▶ a small mirror
- ▶ paper, charcoal, black felt tips and paint

Warm up:

Sit in a circle and play 'Greetings': Use a small ball or bean bag. Say your name and throw the ball gently to a child in the circle. Ask them to try and catch it, say their name and then choose someone else to throw it to. This is a great way of learning names with a new group of children.

- ▶ **Introducing pets** – Go round the circle and invite each child to introduce any pet that they have at home: 'I have a ... and his name is ...'
- ▶ **Show me a feeling** – Pass a small hand mirror round the circle. Invite the children to show an emotion on their face and use the mirror to check. Try happy, sad, angry, tired, calm, brave, scared, worried, naughty, etc. Try again without the mirror and use facial expression and body language to show the different emotions.

▶ **Introduce Sid** – Use a soft toy or puppet to introduce Sid to the children. Explain that he is a very special cat who has six different characters. Make Sid demonstrate some of his different names and characters – Scaramouche, Bob, Satan, Sally, Sooty, Schwartz. Agree that he is a very clever cat!

Story break – Read the story up to where Sid's plan goes wrong because he catches a nasty cough.

▶ **Sid's six characters** – With the help of the illustrations, let children show how they would change their body shape to portray the six different characters of Sid. How would Scaramouche behave that is different from Sally? Can they be 'rough and tough' like Schwartz? Which way would they choose to be scratched? Where would they choose to sleep?'

▶ **Role-play** – Set up a vet's surgery in the role-play area. Create a waiting room with reception desk, telephone, computer screen, appointment diary, leaflets, posters, comfy chairs, animal carry boxes or baskets, etc. Use white shirts or coats for the vet to dress up in and provide some medical equipment, weighing scales, and lots of soft toy animals. Encourage children to role-play the vet seeing Sid six times!

▶ **My poorly pet** – Sing this song to the tune of 'She'll be coming round the mountain':
Better take my poorly pet to the vet, to the vet,
Better take my poorly pet to the vet, to the vet,
Better take my poorly pet, take my poorly pet,
Take my poorly pet, to the vet.

▶ **Role on the wall** – Let children draw a giant picture of Sid the black cat. Scribe different words to describe Sid on post-it notes and stick them on the picture.

▶ **Aristotle Street tableau** – Make a still image of all the six owners who live in Aristotle Street when they find out about Sid's deception! They are furious with him for tricking them. Put Sid the soft toy cat or a confident child pretending to be Sid into the tableau. Repeat the tableau with the owners in Pythagoras Place, who were happy because they knew all about Six Dinner Sid!

▶ **Creative activities** – Draw or paint giant pictures of Sid using charcoal, black felt pens or paint to use in the 'Role on the wall' activity.

Stick Man

by Julia Donaldson

What you need:

- ▶ the book or Stick Man live on stage – www.youtube.com
- ▶ sticks and twigs
- ▶ string/twine/garden wire
- ▶ wooden musical instruments

I will need

Warm up:

Sit the children in a circle and show them a stick. Explain that you are going to play a game of 'Pass the prop' where they take turns to pretend that the stick is not just a stick. They have to mime using the stick as if it were something else such as a pen, brush, sword, knife, umbrella, bat, etc. and the other children must try and guess what the stick has become. Repeat the game with a different-shaped prop such as a saucepan lid or an empty match box.

▶ **Hot seat** – Collect some sticks from outside and create your own Stick Man. Use it as a puppet and interview or hot seat your stick man at different times in the story so far. Let the children ask him questions about how he felt when he gets played with by the dog, thrown into the river, used in the swan's nest or as a flag pole for a sand castle.

▶ **Partner work 1** – Ask children to work with a partner. Let A be the sculptor who has to create a Stick Man out of their partner, B. Encourage the children to allow each other to move their limbs into different positions. Go round and look at all the stick men and see who can stand perfectly still in their new shape. Don't forget to swap over and let the B children have a turn at being sculptors!

▶ **Physical drama** – Play 'Musical Statue Stick Man'. Use some music played on wooden instruments such as 'Music for pieces of wood' by Steve Reich (www.youtube.com) or the children's own music (see below). Every time the music stops invite the children to stop and make the shape of a stick man. Can they make their arms and legs very stiff and spiky?

▶ **Rolling theatre** – In small groups help the children to act out the different scenes from the story. All the children can chant 'I'm Stick Man, I'm Stick Man, I'm Stick Man, that's me!' at the end of each scene. Watch the scenes one by one to create a rolling theatre of the story.

▶ **Chatterpoint** – Talk about how it feels to get lost? What do the children think they should do if they ever get lost?

▶ **Partner work 2** – Work in pairs again and take on the roles of Santa and the Stick Man. Act out the scene when Santa gets stuck up the chimney and needs Stick Man's help.

▶ **Stick men drama** – Let children choose sticks and create their own stick men or stick family. Ask them to use their puppets to talk to each other. Can they make them greet each other and have a conversation or quarrel? Make up a new adventure for the stick men. Invite the children to show their work to the group.

▶ **Creative activities** – Provide the children with lots of different wooden instruments such as claves and woodblocks and let them create their own 'wooden music'.

Dogger

by Shirley Hughes

What you need:

- the book
- a small soft toy or puppet dog

Warm up:

Sit in a circle and hold the toy dog carefully. Stroke him, pretend to whisper to him and make it clear that he is very special. Pass the toy around the circle and let children stroke it and give it a hug. Use this as a sharing time for children to talk about any worries they may have.

– Read the book up to where Dogger goes missing and Dave is feeling desolate.

► **Chatterpoint** – Let children take turns to tell the group about their own special toy. Talk about how it feels when you lose a toy.

► **Hot seating** – Go into role as Dave and let children ask questions about how he feels about Dogger. Ask him how he felt when he realised he had lost Dogger and what he thinks they can do to help find his toy.

► **Hide and seek** – Ask for a volunteer to leave the room and hide the toy dog somewhere in the room. When the child comes back in let the other children guide them to the hiding place using 'hot' and 'cold' or clapping quieter and louder. How does it feel when the toy is found again?

Story break – Read on up to where Dave sees Dogger on the toy stall at the fair. Do the children think there will be a happy ending. Read the rest of the story.

► **Looking for Dogger** – Sit in a circle and take turns to think of somewhere Dave and his family looked for Dogger. Try to accumulate the places so that the list gets longer and longer each time. Who can remember the most places? Act out the search using children as characters and places!

► **Teacher in role** – Go into role as Bella. Let children ask her about how she felt when Dave lost Dogger. And later how she felt when she wins the big teddy and decides to swop it for Dogger.

► **Role-play** – Set up a school fair or fête in the role-play area with different types of stalls – toys, books, tombola, how many sweets in the jar, name the teddy, guess the weight of the cake, find the treasure on the map, etc. Ask children to go into role as people at the fair working at stalls or trying out different games and buying things.

► **Still image** – Using the toy stall as a background, build up a still image of the scene where Bella hands over her newly won big yellow teddy with the blue silk bow to the little girl in order to get Dogger back. Invite three children to play the roles of Bella, Dave and the little girl. Add them to the scene one at a time, look at the pictures in the story and ask them to think of what each character might do or say. Let other children tap them on the shoulder and invite them to say what they are feeling. Scribe it into speech bubbles.

► **Creative activities** – Let children help make resources for the role-play school fair.

Knock Knock Who's There?

by Sally Grindley

What you need:

▶ the book

▶ a collection of hats (baseball cap, top, flat cap, cowboy, witch, flowery, beret, crown, woolly, sunhat, helmet, Muslim cap, etc.)

Warm up:

Sit in a circle and place a collection of different hats in the middle. Let children take turns to choose a hat and then walk around the circle in character.

▶ **Drama bodies** – This game is an exercise in using posture and body language to portray a character. Ask children to think about how a King or Queen would move. Then change it to a beggar or burglar. Compare how a young and old person move. Try contrasting characters such as a floppy rag doll and a stiff robot. Invite the children to suggest other characters they can mime with their bodies.

- ▶ **One-line characters** – Sit in a circle and choose three or four characters such as 'angry teacher', 'sad parent', 'grumpy grandmother' or 'happy shopkeeper'. Invite children to stand up and say one line that they think the character might say. Provide a suitable line if the children need help. Can the other children guess which character they are pretending to be? Remind them to use appropriate body language as well as words.

Story break – Read the story and make a list of all the characters who knock at the door.

- ▶ **Character corners** – Clearly label the four corners of the room 1–4. Ask children to choose one of the characters from the story and move around the room in character. Think about speed, style and dynamic of the movement. Play fun music for them to move to and make suggestions to improve their characterisations. Turn away, stop the music and ask children to move silently to one of the corners. Call out a number and all the children who are in that corner are out and can help you with the next round.

- ▶ **Knock knock** – If possible use a real door and let a confident child go outside the door and knock. Invite another child to open the door and see who is pretending to be there. It can be a character from the story or one of their own choosing.

- ▶ **Partner work 1** – Ask children to choose a partner to work with. Invite them to take turns being the person who opens the door while the other mimes a character from the story or from their imagination. Go round watching the pairs working and select pairs to show their work to the rest of the group.

- ▶ **What happens next?** – Go through the story and as each character comes to the door – gorilla, witch, ghost, dragon, giant – talk about what the little girl imagines might happen next. Let the children use their imaginations to think about what else might happen.

- ▶ **Partner work 2** – Ask children to work with a partner to act out short scenes using their imaginary ideas from 'what happens next?' Take turns to be the little girl and her surprise visitors.

- ▶ **Wind down** – Sit in a circle and let the children share who they would most like to be behind the door when it knocks.

- ▶ **Creative activities** – Play a game of 'Misfits' using a mixture of hat, face, body, and legs cards to create mixed up characters.

Beegu

by Alexis Deacon

What you need:

▶ the book
▶ an echo microphone
▶ a hula hoop
▶ materials for the planet surface

Warm up:

Introduce the character of Beegu. Show children the picture in the book where Beegu's speech bubble is full of random marks. Invite them to make up their own alien language. Pass the alien sounds round the circle using an echo microphone. Talk about intonation, changes in pitch, nonsense words, etc.

▶ **Chatterpoint** – Talk about being lost like Beegu. Invite the children to share their experiences and memories of being lost. How does it feel? What should you do if you get lost?

▶ **Guided tour** – Take the children on a guided tour of the different locations at the beginning of the book. Walk round and describe them, encouraging the children to use their imaginations. Alternatively, use pictures of scenes from the book blown up on the IWB.

▶ **Role on the wall** – Blow up a giant picture of Beegu and display on the wall. Help children to scribe words to describe her on post-it notes and stick on the picture. Repeat at different stages of the story.

▶ **Physical drama** – Ask children to move around like Beegu. Can they make their faces, bodies and movement seem sad, lost and uncertain? Then change and contrast with the busy, confident people bustling around in the street scene. Try switching between the two moods and movements. Add suitable contrasting music.

Story break – Read to the end of the story when Beegu is reunited with his parents.

▶ **Group still images** – Use the book to help the children make still images of these scenes: Beegu and the children, Beegu and the teacher, Beegu and the hula hoop. Perform the still images in sequence as a rolling theatre. Use thought tracking to find out what the characters are thinking.

▶ **Role-play** – Set up an alien planet surface in the role-play area. Cover large tyres in drapes to create craters. Hang up dark curtains as the space backdrop. Attach silver stars onto the curtains. Provide space suits and helmets for the children to dress up in. Make oxygen tanks from empty two litre plastic bottles. Invite children to pretend to land on the planet and explore just like Beegu did on earth. What will they find? Will they be able to communicate? Encourage children to imagine and devise dramatic scenes on the planet.

▶ **Creative activities** – Build a giant rocket out of cardboard boxes covered in aluminium foil. Add buttons and dials using coloured plastic lids.

Bringing Down the Moon

by Jonathan Emmett

What you need:

- ▶ the book
- ▶ a soft toy or puppet mole
- ▶ peaceful music and a player
- ▶ a lamp

Warm up:

Make the room as dark as possible and ask children to find a space in the room. Play some peaceful music such as Beethoven's 'Moonlight sonata' and ask them to move around the room carefully in the dark as though they were nocturnal animals. Without warning, switch on a lamp in the corner of the room to represent the moon. Ask the children to sit still by the light of the moon. Can they think of words to describe the moon?

Story break – Read the beginning of the story when Mole first sees the moon.

- ▶ **Chatterpoint** – Talk about things that the children would really like to touch, catch, see or feel. Have they ever wondered about the sun, moon or stars like Mole?

▶ **Blind mole walks** – Ask children to work with a partner. Each pair takes turns to close their eyes or wear a blindfold and let their partner lead them around the room avoiding obstacles and other children. Every now and then stop and ask the children to open their eyes. What is the first thing they see?

Story break – Read up to where Mole falls out of the tree. Talk about the different characters in the story.

▶ **Physical drama** – Make a list of all the different actions Mole tries to bring down the moon: digging, jumping, poking with a stick, throwing acorns, climbing a tree, falling in a puddle... Help the children to mime the actions in sequence.

▶ **It's not as near as it looks** – Let children work with a partner. One takes on the role of Mole and the other either Rabbit, Hedgehog or Squirrel. Help them to create the three different scenes with these characters as Mole tries out his ideas to catch the moon. Choose three pairs to tell the story as a rolling theatre. At the end of each scene all the children can chorus 'It's not as near as it looks'.

Story break – Read to the end of the story.

▶ **Hot seat** – Go into role as Mole or use a soft toy or puppet. Let the children ask him questions about how he feels at different points in the story. Compare his feelings when he thinks he has broken the moon with how he feels at the end of the story.

▶ **Reflections** – Ask children to work with a partner and play 'Mirrors'. Take turns to be the mirror and the subject. Try changing body shapes for their partner to copy, then pull faces, mime different actions from the story and finally 'break'.

▶ **Improvisation** – Talk about how it feels to break something such as a toy, cup, piece of equipment, etc. Make up a story about something being broken and allow children to use their ideas to improvise a drama. What will be broken and how? Will it be someone's fault or an accident? How will the drama end?

▶ **Creative activities** – Make a moon to hang up in your setting using a huge cardboard circle covered with different white, silver and gold materials and paint.

Little Beaver and The Echo

by Amy MacDonald

What you need:

▶ the book
▶ a boat or box
▶ a beanbag, ball, soft toy beaver
▶ two tin cans, paper cups and string

Warm up:

Sit in a circle and ask children to copy you. Clap a simple pattern and ask them to echo it. Try singing a simple pattern using the two cuckoo notes. Use the word 'soh' for the high note and 'me' for the lower note.

► **Meet and greet** – Ask children to find a space in the room. Invite them to move around while you shake a tambourine taking care not to bump into each other. When they hear you tap the tambourine they must stop and 'meet and greet' the nearest person in different ways. Try shaking hands, bowing and curtseying, hugging, high-fiving, etc.

Story break – Read the story up to where Little Beaver gets into his boat to go and find a friend.

► **Chatterpoint** – Talk about feeling lonely with the children. What do they do when they feel lonely?

► **Follow my leader** – Choose a child to be Little Beaver and take the lead. As he rows across the pond try singing this song to the tune of 'Row row row the boat':

Beaver rows the boat,
Off to find a friend.
Will he find one, will he find one
Before the story ends?

Ask another child to take the part of Duck and join Little Beaver in his boat by following him around and singing the song again. Then add in Otter and Squirrel, singing each time.

Story break – Read the story to the end. Had the children guessed who the Echo was?

► **Wise old beaver says** – Play a version of 'Simon says' using 'Wise Old Beaver' at the front of each instruction. Remind the children not to copy the action if you do not preface it with 'Wise Old Beaver'.

► **Partner work** – Ask children to choose a partner and then stand far apart either in the room or outside. Invite them to take turns in shouting messages across the room for their partner to 'echo'. Alternatively, use two tin cans or paper cups stretched between a long piece of string to create a phone and let the pairs send messages to each other.

► **Throw that feeling** – Sit in a circle and throw a beanbag or soft toy to a child. Shout out a feeling such as sad, happy, angry, worried, tired, scared, etc. and ask them to mime the appropriate face. Then ask them to throw the toy to another child in the circle, shout out a different feeling and continue the game.

► **Creative activities** – Use a huge cardboard box to construct a boat to use in the drama. Cut the boat down to look like the canoe in the story. Ask children to paint the box in bright colours.

Pumpkin Soup

by Helen Cooper

What you need:

▶ the book
▶ a wooden spoon
▶ a large cooking pot
▶ animal puppets

Warm up:

Ask children to sit in a circle and pass a wooden spoon around as they sing this song to the tune of 'London Bridge':

Pass the spoon round the ring,
Round the ring, round the ring,
Pass the spoon round the ring,
What's it going to be?

Whoever is holding the spoon at the end mimes using the spoon as a 'prop'. Can the children use the spoon as though it is a brush, pencil, drum stick, knife, ruler, walking stick, etc. Encourage them to use their imagination and invite others to guess the identity of the prop from the mime.

Story break – Read the beginning of the story up to where 'Everyone is happy'.

▶ **Making soup** – Talk through the process of making soup from the book – slicing the pumpkin, heating and stirring the water and adding just the right amount of salt. Ask children to mime each stage. How will they prepare the pumpkin? Talk about peeling, deseeding, chopping and slicing and the different movements they require. Will they stir the soup in a big or small pot? Can they stir faster or slower? How much salt will they add? Encourage them to use their hands carefully to show a 'pipkin of salt'.

Story break – Read up to where the fight breaks out and Duck storms off.

▶ **Hot seat** – Hot seat each of the three characters in turn, going into the role yourself or using puppets or confident children. Compare the characters' behaviour at the beginning when all seems calm, with the part where Duck wants a turn stirring the soup and a fight breaks out.

Story break – Read to the end of the story. Talk about taking turns.

▶ **Rolling theatre** – In groups of three, invite children to take turns to act out the characters of Cat, Squirrel and Duck at different stages of the book such as the opening, the fight, and the reunion at the end. Talk about feelings and how to show them using facial expression and body language.

▶ **Follow my leader** – Cat and Squirrel have to go out looking for Duck who has waddled off after the fight. Take turns to be the leader looking in the pumpkin patch, walking through the dark woods, scrambling down the steep cliff, etc.

▶ **Thought tracking** – Set out the final scene of the book as a freeze frame. Cat, Squirrel and Duck have changed roles. Hold speech or thought bubbles over each character and let children say their thoughts for them. Scribe them in the bubbles. What do the children think might happen next...?

▶ **Role-play** – Set up the home corner as the old white cabin. Provide a tin whistle and a banjo for the Cat and Squirrel to play. Put a large cooking pot, spoon, bowls and other cooking equipment in the kitchen. Make up one bed with a duvet. Let children dress up as the characters using masks (see below) and fur waist coats. Allow them opportunities to role-play different parts of the story.

▶ **Creative activities** – Make simple masks for the animals to wear using outlines, covered with fun fur fabric, wool, paint, feathers, etc.

Cook some home made pumpkin soup with the children. Make sure everyone has a turn at stirring the soup!

Oliver's Vegetables

by Vivian French

What you need:

- ▶ the book
- ▶ real or toy vegetables from the story

Warm up:

Go round the circle and give each child the name of one of the vegetables from the story – carrots, spinach, beetroot, peas, cabbage, etc. Ask them to change places each time you call out the name of their vegetable. If you call out 'Vegetable soup!' all the children must change places!

Story break – Read the book showing the children the actual vegetable at each point in the story. Ask them if they have tried each vegetable.

▶ **Chatterpoint** – Talk about the children's experiences with their grandparents. What do they like to do when they visit them?

- **Mime mirrors** – Ask children to choose a partner. Invite them to choose a type of food they like to eat and one they dislike. Ask them to take turns miming eating each of the food types. Can their partner guess what they are eating and if they like it or not? To improve the mimes, encourage them to think carefully about how they eat each food. Do they need to chew, suck, peel or bite?

- **Role on wall** – Draw round a boy and paint the figure to look like Oliver. Display the picture on the wall and scribe words to describe Oliver at the beginning of the story and then again at the end. Does he change during the story?

- **Physical drama** – Ask children to pretend to be Oliver looking for different vegetables. When he finds each one, how does he pick, pull or dig it up? Practise miming for each vegetable – cutting spinach, pulling up carrots, picking peapods, and digging up potatoes. Which tools will they need to use?

- **Partner work** – Ask children to choose a partner to work with. Decide who is going to be Oliver and who is going to be Grandpa. Let them choose a day from the story to act out finding a different vegetable to try.

- **Story sequence** – Choose a pair of children for each day of the week and ask them to perform their scene as part of a rolling theatre. The other children can recite the words each time e.g. 'On Monday, Oliver ate some carrots'.

- **Hot seat** – Go into role as Grandpa. Let children ask him questions about the story. Did he plan to trick Oliver into eating lots of different vegetables?

- **I am your Grandpa** – Sing this song to the tune of 'I am the music man'. Use the repeated letter sounds to practise phonics.

  I am your grandpa,
  I like to grow my own.
  What shall I grow?
  I just don't know!

  P-p-p-p-p-p-peas,
  P-p-peas, p-p-peas,
  P-p-p-p-p-p-peas,
  P-p-p-p-peas.
  (carrots, beetroot, potatoes)

- **Role-play** – Set up a garden in the role-play area. Place real and pretend vegetables, flowers and plants, etc. on a brown mat or large sheets of corrugated cardboard. Provide gardening tools, watering cans, seed packets, wheel barrows, gloves and boots. Let children use the story as inspiration for imaginative play.

Mr Benn

by David McKee

What you need:

▶ the book or dvd of the cartoon
▶ lots of dressing up clothes
▶ a prop bag full of suitable props

I will need

Warm up:

Sit in a circle and place a selection of different dressing up items in the middle – hats, shoes, etc. Try singing this song to the tune of 'In and out the dusky bluebells' as you pass round a bean bag:

Pick a hat/shoe and put it on, x3
Who will you become?
Whoever is holding the bean bag at the end of the song can choose a hat or shoe and become a 'character'.

▶ **Prop bag** – Make a collection of items that could be used as props such as a telephone, bag, keys, tickets, purse, whistle, handcuffs, newspaper, sun glasses, egg cup, pen, sword, book, jewellery, etc. Put them all in a suitcase or big bag and invite children to take turns to pick a prop out of the bag and pretend to use it. Can they think of a line of dialogue that they could say while using each prop?

Story break – Introduce the character of Mr Benn through one of his extraordinary adventures (in a book or on dvd).

▶ **Chatterpoint** – Talk about all the different characters Mr Benn dresses up as in the stories – cook, caveman, hunter, zookeeper, diver, cowboy, pirate, spaceman, knight, clown, wizard, and gladiator. Which characters would the children like to dress up as? Have they got a favourite costume?

▶ **Role-play** – Set up the role-play area as the little shop 'with all sorts of interesting things to wear'. Use a table as a counter, and provide a changing room with a curtain and a mirror. Encourage children to choose different outfits to put on and to act out some of Mr Benn's adventures.

▶ **Partner work** – Ask children to work with a partner and take turns at being Mr Benn and the shopkeeper. Use polite language from the book such as 'Can I help you, sir?' and 'I'd like to try the 'space man's suit', etc.

▶ **A letter from Mr Benn** – Explain that you have had a letter from Mr Benn asking the children to help him in his next adventure. Read out the letter :

Dear children

My name is Mr Benn. You may have read some of my adventures? Unfortunately, I am stuck in the land of fancy dress and can't find my way back. I need your help!

Love from Mr Benn.

Invite a group of children to dress up in the fancy dress of their choice and then go through the door in the changing room (see 'Role-play') to find Mr Benn. How will they tell which of the characters in fancy dress land is Mr Benn if they are all dressed up in costume? Go into role as Mr Benn wearing his bowler hat and greet some of the children. Can they show Mr Benn the way home?

▶ **As if by magic** – Talk about other imaginary lands that Mr Benn could go to. Invite children to draw some magical settings for a new Mr Benn story. Create a story map with the children for the new story. What costume will he wear? Who will he meet? What extraordinary adventure will he have? Act out the new story.

Where's My Teddy?

by Jez Alborough

What you need:

- ▶ the book
- ▶ lots of different-sized teddy bears
- ▶ a triangle and drum

Warm up:

Invite all the children to bring in a special teddy bear from home. Help them to make a name label for their bear. Go round the circle and ask each child to introduce themselves and their bear to the group. Can they think of one reason why their bear is special?

▶ **Teddy hide and seek** – Ask for a volunteer to leave the room while their bear is hidden by another child. Can they return and try to find their bear? The seeker can be guided by the other children singing this song to the tune of 'London Bridge':

(Seeker's name)'s teddy is hiding,

Hiding, hiding.

(Seeker's name)'s teddy is hiding,

Where can he be?

When the seeker is near the hiding place, the children should sing louder and when far from the hiding place the song should be quieter.

▶ **The woods** – Show the children a large scale picture of the opening double spread in the book on the IWB to introduce the story. Darken the room and ask children to share their thoughts and feelings as they imagine themselves in the wood. What do they think they will find in the wood?

Story break – Turn over the pages and introduce Eddy as he goes into the woods to find his teddy. Read on to where Eddy finds a giant teddy bear. Can the children guess what has happened? How has Eddy's teddy got so big?

▶ **Hot seat** – Invite a child to go into role as Eddy and let others ask him how he is feeling. Use the biggest teddy available as a puppet and ask him what has happened. How did he get lost?

Story break – Read the rest of the story. Did any of the children guess that the giant teddy belonged to someone else?

▶ **Physical drama** – Ask children to pretend to be Eddy tip-toeing through the wood, stopping every now and then to listen. Let him find the biggest teddy bear and say 'You're too big to huddle and cuddle'. Then ask children to imagine that they are the real bear in the story. How will they move about the wood? Suggest moving slowly, stomping, taking large steps, sobbing and crying out 'You're too small to huddle and cuddle' in a growly bear voice. Find some tiny teddy bears for the children to carry as they go. Emphasise the contrasting movements. Signal the change with quiet delicate taps on the triangle for Eddy and loud bangs on a drum for the bear.

▶ **Partner work** – Ask children to work with a partner and recreate the meeting between the boy and the bear! Choose pairs to act out the scene to the rest of the group, the moment when Eddy meets the real bear and reclaims his tiny teddy. Can they run away through the dark woods back to their beds!

▶ **Creative activities** – Make bear masks for the children to use in their drama.

Oi! Get Off Our Train

by John Burningham

What you need:

▶ the book

▶ soft toy animals or puppets

I will need

Warm up:

Try some echo clapping. Invite the children to copy simple 4-beat patterns. Then ask the children to clap and say the words 'Off our train' over and over again to create an 'ostinato' (repeated pattern) to sound like the rhythm of a train.

▶ **All change** – Stand in a circle and give each child the name of a local place. Ask the station master to stand in the middle with a list of all the places on a clipboard and then call out two place names: 'The train from Northampton to London'. The children with those names swap places. The station master tries to steal one of their places. Try shouting 'All change!' and all the children have to change places.

▶ **Chatterpoint** – Talk about bedtime routines. Which toys do the children like to take to bed with them?

▶ **Endangered animals parade** – Sit in a circle and make a list of all the animals who tried to board the train – elephant, seal, crane, tiger, polar bear. Invite children to show different ways of miming each of these animals. How will they move like an elephant – slow and lumbering, seal – flapping flippers, crane – flying with wings outstretched, tiger – stalking, polar bear – rearing up on hind legs?

▶ **Rolling theatre** – Construct a train using stage blocks or play equipment. Choose five children from the parade to be each of the animals trying to get on the train. Of the remaining children, invite pairs of children to be the boy and his pyjama dog shouting at all the animals. Help them to use the words from the book. Create a sequence or rolling theatre of the scenes as the train gets fuller.

▶ **Chatterpoint** – Talk about endangered animals. Find out about other endangered animals and organisations that help them.

▶ **Weather forecasts** – After each animal has said their lines look at the illustrations with the children and see if they can guess or remember what the weather is going to be like. Foggy – play ghosts, hot – go for a swim, windy – fly kites, rain – muck about with umbrellas, snow – throw snowballs. Have fun miming each of the activities.

▶ **Follow my leader** – Ask the children to stand in a long line like a train, with their hands around each others waists. The child at the beginning of the line must lead the others around. Ask an animal from the parade (see above) to take turns to join the train. Place children around the room to mime the different weather dreams as the train passes by.

▶ **Chatterpoint** – Talk to the children about dreams. Can they remember any of their dreams?

▶ **Role-play the ending** – Set up the home corner as the bedroom with a bed, duvet, and pillows. Provide pyjamas, slippers, pyjama cases, teddy bears, etc. Add a train set and plastic or soft toy animals – elephant, seal, bird, tiger, and polar bear. Encourage the children to hide the animals around the area as at the end of the book.

The Bad-Tempered Ladybird

by Eric Carle

What you need:

▶ the book
▶ finger puppet ladybirds
▶ red and black felt
▶ wood block and bells

> ## Warm up:
>
> Ask children to stand in a circle and begin to conduct the 'I've got a feeling' band. Ask the first three children to make faces and noises as though they are sad, the next three happy, the next three angry and the next three scared, and so on. Go round each group varying the dynamics, i.e. loud and quiet, try with all the groups together or one at a time.

> **Story break** – Introduce the bad tempered ladybird as a finger puppet or soft toy. Read the story up to where she flies off to find someone bigger to fight!

▶ **Partner work** – Use the dialogue on the second double page to create a partner drama between the pairs of children taking on the roles of the friendly ladybird and the bad-tempered ladybird. Encourage them to use suitable voices and body language to emphasise the different personalities of their ladybirds.

▶ **At six o'clock** – Use two-tone wood blocks and bells to create the sound of a clock ticking and chiming the hours throughout the book. Chime an o'clock and see if the children can count what time it is.

Story break – Read the rest of the story up to where the bad-tempered ladybird meets the whale. What do the children think will happen now?

▶ **Timed lists** – Sit in a circle and challenge the children to remember and make a list of the animals in the story. Can they also remember the time that each animal meets the ladybird?

▶ **Animal ambush** – Try these movement ideas based on the game of 'Beans', involving all the animals that the bad-tempered ladybird meets. Encourage the children to come up with ideas for each animal and then choose the best one for the game. Here are some ideas to start off with: wasp – run around buzzing with finger pointing behind like a sting; stag beetle – walk around with arms opening and closing like jaws; praying mantis – kneel down with arms outstretched; sparrow – run around with arms out like wings; and so on. Use the times to signal the different animals so number two is the 'gorilla' and number eleven is the 'skunk'.

▶ **Rolling theatre** – Ask children to work with a partner and act out the different encounters between the ladybird and the different animals. Choose pairs to perform each scene and produce the story as a rolling theatre.

▶ **The ladybird and the whale** – Read the end of the story. Try this physical drama. Ask all the children to stand in pairs holding hands in a long line to represent the huge blue whale. Help them to lift their hands and send a ripple down the line as the whale swims along. Invite one child to take on the role of the bad-tempered ladybird flying the length of the whale. Use a finger puppet (see below) and move very slowly. The pair of children at the tail end can tap the finger puppet into the air with a SLAP!

▶ **Creative activities** – Make ladybird finger puppets from tips of knitted gloves cut off or red felt circles with black felt spots stuck on. Let the children decide if their ladybird is friendly or bad-tempered.

The Rainbow Fish

by Marcus Pfister

What you need:

- ▶ the book
- ▶ a soft toy fish
- ▶ shiny scales cut out of card
- ▶ the music 'Aquarium' from 'Carnival of the Animals' by Saint Saens and player

Warm up:

Sit in a circle and pass round the soft toy fish. Let the children take turns to share news with the group while holding the fish. If they don't want to share just pass the fish on to the next child.

▶ **Feelings forum** – Make a list of different feelings. Encourage children to try and think of a feeling that no one else has named. Can they show the different feelings in their facial expression or body language?

▶ **In the swim** – Invite children to swim around like fish to the music of 'Aquarium' from Saint Saens 'Carnival of the Animals'. When the music stops ask them to pair off with the nearest child to them. Ask them to take turns to show their partner how they are feeling using facial expressions, body language and words.

Story break – Introduce the Rainbow Fish. Read the story up to where the Rainbow Fish goes to visit the Wise Octopus.

▶ **Chatterpoint** – Talk about why the Rainbow Fish is feeling sad. He is lonely because he thinks he is too beautiful to swim with the other fish. Link the loneliness he feels with the refusal to share.

▶ **Hot seat** – Go into role as the Rainbow Fish using a soft toy or puppet. Let the children ask questions and find out more about what the fish is thinking at different times in the story.

▶ **Role on the wall** – Blow up a picture of the Rainbow Fish from the book and display on the wall. Alternatively, create a giant collage of the Fish using individual scales decorated by the children. Let the children choose words to describe the fish to write on paper and add to the picture. Will their words change as the story continues?

Story break – Read the meeting between the Rainbow Fish and the Wise Octopus. What do the children think the Rainbow Fish will do? Read onto the end of the story.

▶ **Partner work** – Ask children to work with a partner and take turns to be the Rainbow Fish and the Wise Octopus. What would the Wise Octopus like to say to the Rainbow Fish?

▶ **In the swim again** – Move around to the same music as before. This time when the music stops ask all the children to stop as though in a freeze frame. Nominate one child to be the Rainbow Fish and to keep moving in and out of the picture as they give every other child a shiny scale to hold.

▶ **A very peculiar feeling** – The Rainbow Fish feels different when he has shared his beautiful scales. Invite children to bring in special toys from home to share and play with a friend. Share a snack together (see below).

▶ **Creative activities** – Make a giant Rainbow Fish pizza to share with a ready-made base and scales made from slices of mushroom, pepperoni, tomato and mozzarella cheese.

Stories from around the world

Anansi the Spider

African traditional tale

What you need:

▶ the book or story
▶ black pompoms, egg boxes, black paint, black pipe cleaners

Warm up:

Sing the rhyme 'Little Miss Muffet' and let children show how they look when frightened. Use a spider puppet or homemade spider (see page 73). Can children choose a different feeling to show when the spider sits down beside them – happy, sad, angry, calm, excited, worried?

▶ **Pass the spider** – Sit in a circle and pretend to hold a spider in the palm of your hand. Show children by how you move where the spider is crawling, hanging, spinning. Then pass it very carefully to a confident child and let them hold it and repeat.

Story break – Read the beginning of the story and introduce Anansi and his six sons. Stop at the point where Anansi gets lost and falls into trouble.

▶ **Six spiders** – Explain to the children that each time you call out one of the spider's names they are going to do a different action: 'See Trouble' – put hand up over top of eyes as though looking into the distance; 'Road Builder' – mime building with bricks by piling fists on top of each other; 'River Drinker' – mime drinking from a huge cup; 'Game Skinner' – mime holding a knife and slicing the air; 'Stone Thrower' – mime throwing a stone high into the sky; 'Cushion' – sit down. See how quickly the children can react as you call out the different names.

▶ **Physical drama** – Choose a child to be Anansi and play 'Follow my leader'. Ask Anansi to lead the other children in a long line as they walk over the mountains, through the forest, over the cliff, into the river, swim inside the fish, fly in the sky, fall to the ground, etc.

▶ **Role court** – Go into role as Nyame, the God of All Things. Help Anansi to decide which of his six sons saved him and deserves the gift of the moon. Let each son come forward and say how he helped save his father Anansi.

▶ **Pass the moon** – Use a big white or yellow ball as the moon and throw it to a child. If they catch it they can say the name of one of the six sons and everyone has do the actions (see 'Six spiders' above). Then the child must pass the moon to another child.

▶ **Creative activities** – Use black pompoms or paint an egg box segment black to create a model spider. Add legs made out of black pipe cleaners or black velvet ribbon. Attach a piece of elastic so the spider can jump and dance about.

Try some spider dancing. Choose some bouncy music such as a Tarantella – a fast moving dance supposed to be inspired by the bite of a spider! The children can make their spider models dance or dance themselves!

The Five Magic Brothers

Chinese folk tale

What you need:

▶ the book or story
▶ a balloon

Warm up:

Ask children to move around the room, carefully weaving in and out of each other. When you shout out a number they must get into groups of that number as quickly as possible. Start with twos, then threes, fours and finally fives. Encourage the groups to have a group hug as they wait for the signal to move on.

▶ **Balloons** – Blow up a balloon until it is fully expanded and then let the air out slowly. Let children copy this with their faces and bodies growing fat and round like an inflated balloon and then slowly deflating. At the end of the activity let go of the balloon and it will whiz wildly round the room as it deflates. Let the children copy this movement.

Story break – Read the story and introduce the five identical Chinese brothers and their magic powers.

▶ **Pass the face** – Sit in a circle and slowly make a funny face. Turn slowly to the child next to you and ask them to copy or mirror your face exactly. They can then slowly change and make their own funny face and turn to the child next to them who copies it. Try to do this game in slow motion and emphasise that the faces must be as identical as possible before they are changed.

▶ **Physical drama** – Ask children to find a space to stand in. Introduce the five brothers and their magical powers. When you call out '1' or hold up a thumb the children must pretend to be the first brother and mime swallowing lots of water, then puffing out their cheeks, pretending to swell up and finally letting the water all spray out! When you call out '2' or hold up your pointing finger children must mime the second brother's magic power – walking around very stiffly as though their necks are made of metal! Hold up your index finger or call out '3' and the children must pretend to dance around very fast avoiding the hot coals and flames as they can't be burned. The fourth brother can hold his breath so ask the children to stand still, breathe in and hold their breath as long as they can when you hold up your ring finger or call out '4'. When you call out '5' or hold up your little finger the children must stretch their arms in the air and stretch their legs as far apart as possible.

▶ **Rolling theatre** – Act out the five scenes as the five brothers each come before the judge and executioner and then put together as rolling theatre to tell the story.

▶ **Happy endings** – Create a freeze frame at the end of the rolling theatre with the five brothers at home with their mother and their pockets full of gold. Tap each brother on the shoulder and ask them to tell their part of the story.

The Pea Blossom

Hans Christian Andersen

What you need:

- ▶ the book or story
- ▶ xylophone and drum
- ▶ green tissue and sugar paper

Warm up:

Sit in a circle and pass around a fresh pea pod for children to handle and smell. Show them how to pop the pod open and share out the peas inside. Say the finger rhyme 'Five fat peas in a peapod pressed'.

Story break – Read or tell the story up to where the peas have all shared their dreams for the future.

▶ **What's my line?** – Let the children share what they would like to be when they grow up. Try out some mimes of different jobs such as teacher, bus driver, shop assistant, doctor, hairdresser, etc. Help the children think of different things to do for the mimes and improve their skills. Invite confident child to mime a job for the others to identify.

▶ **Physical drama** – Ask children to find a space in the room and curl up small like a tiny pea. Play the xylophone, starting at the lowest note and slowly moving up to the highest note. As the music grows higher can they stretch out the fingers on one hand, then the other and then stretch out their arms like branches on a pea plant? Instruct them to gradually stand up tall and make their fingers spikey to look like flowers. When the music stops, ask them to stand up straight and tall with fingers and toes pressed together like a pea pod. Make a loud sound on a drum as the pea pod pops and the story starts again.

Story break – Read or tell the rest of the story and find out what happens to each of the five peas after they are shot out of the boy's peashooter.

▶ **Pea numbers 1-5** – Try this action game. Call out different numbers from 1-5 and make up actions to mime who catches the peas. 1 – fly like a bird and pick up the pea? 2 – jump like a frog and eat the pea; 3 and 4 – move slowly and regally like an Emperor, before eating rice with chopsticks; 5 – bounce, curl up small and then, grow!

▶ **Rolling theatre** – In small groups retell the story or fate of each pea. The first lands in a gutter and is eaten by a pigeon. The second lands in a dark well and is eaten by a frog. The third and fourth land in a dish of rice and are served to the Emperor for his dinner. And the final fifth pea lands on the windowsill of a small house where it grows into a plant. Watch the scenes one by one to create a rolling theatre.

▶ **Hot seat** – Go into role as the young girl. Answer the children's questions about how she felt when she first saw the little pea plant. Why did the plant make a difference? Add a final scene and happy ending to the rolling theatre.

▶ **Creative activities** – Let the children make their own pea pods with green sugar paper. Show them how to cut a hinged pea pod from a folded piece of paper. Stick in five fat tissue paper peas. Can they use this to tell the story to a friend?

The Drum

Indian folk tale

What you need:

- ▶ the book or story
- ▶ a stick or twig
- ▶ a musical drum
- ▶ props – bread, pot, clothes, hobby horse

Warm up:

Practise playing simple rhythm patterns on a small drum for the children to clap back or echo. Pass the drum around the circle and let children take turns to make up a pattern. Can they play the rhythm of their name for everyone to copy? To choose who is going to play use this song to the tune of 'Hot cross buns' as you pass the drum:

Pass the drum,
Pass the drum,
Pass the drum around the ring,
Pass the drum.

Story break – Read or tell the story up to where the strange little man gives the boy's mother a stick. Can the children guess how the stick will help the little boy get his secret wish?

▶ **Secret wishes** – Ask the children to sit in a circle and to share their secret wishes. Pass the magic stick around the children and invite them to only speak when holding it. If they can't think of a wish to share they can pass the stick to the next person.

▶ **Magic stick** – Pass the stick round the circle and on a given signal such as a bell ringing the child holding it must pretend it has turned into something else. Can they mime using the new prop and see if the others can guess what it has become?

Story break – Read the rest of the story and make a list of all the meetings and exchanges which take place as the stick works its magic! Make a collection of props from the story.

▶ **Rolling theatre** – Divide the children into groups to act out each of the five scenes – the old woman who needs wood and gives the boy some bread; the potter's wife who needs bread and gives the boy a pot; the washer man who needs a pot and gives the boy his coat; the naked man who needs clothes and gives the boy his horse; the wedding party who need a horse and give the boy a drum! Use the scenes in a rolling theatre to tell the story.

▶ **Teacher in role** – Go into role as the boy and talk about how it felt to help all those people and then be rewarded with your secret wish at the end.

▶ **Physical drama** – Choose a child to be the boy and play Follow my leader. Lead the children around the room visiting the old woman, the potter's wife, the washer man, the naked man and the wedding party. Use ideas from the book to describe the setting as the game proceeds.

▶ **Indian dance** – Listen to some Indian drumming (tabla) and watch some Indian dancing online. Celebrate the boy getting his drum and try some simple drumming patterns and dance steps.

▶ **Creative activities** – Make drums using different-sized biscuit or sweet tins. Stretch electrical or masking tape over the open end in a criss cross pattern until it is completely covered. Stick paper or sticky plastic around the outside of the cylinder to decorate.

Bringing the Rain to Kapiti Plain

Verna Aardema (African traditional tale)

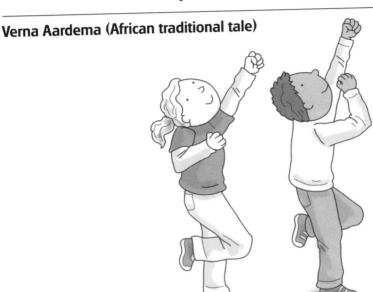

What you need:

- ▶ the book or story
- ▶ some feathers
- ▶ musical instruments to create rain music

Warm up:

Give every child a feather and stand in a space in the room. Ask them to throw the feathers up into the air and watch them float down. Each time, challenge them to catch the feather on a different part of their body such as hand, foot, arm, head, nose, etc. Can the children fall to the ground as though they are as light as a feather?

▶ **Guided tour** – Lead the children around the room describing the Kapiti plain. Display a picture of the plains from the book or an African photo on the IWB. Point out the fresh green grass, nesting birds and the acacia trees providing shade for the animals and leaves for the giraffes. Describe the animals – giraffe, cows, leopards, zebra, birds, ostrich, etc.

Story break – Read the introduction and then pause. What happened to the plain when the rain stopped? Ask the children if they can guess how Ki-pat and a feather can change the weather? Continue to read the rest of the story.

▶ **Memory game** – Sit in a circle and ask children to help you to make a list of the sequence of characters or events – cloud, grass, cows, Ki-pat, eagle, arrow, bow, shot, etc.

▶ **Dramatic verse** – This sort of accumulative story in verse is a good way for children to experience learning words and reciting them. Give four lines about each of the characters or events (see above) to eight groups of children and ask them to learn to say them out loud together. Rehearse each group saying their words to create the accumulative story. Emphasise the importance of projecting their words and speaking clearly and loudly. Everybody can say the final two verses together. Perform the poem to an audience.

▶ **Physical drama** – Ask the children to find a space in the room. Invite them to try standing on one leg like Ki-pat. How long can they balance for? Stand on the other leg. Which is the most stable? Can they hop around the room? Then try miming making the arrow using a slender stick and the eagle feather. And finally shooting the arrow at the cloud. Play some rain music (see below).

▶ **Creative activities** – Make arrows using twigs or sticks and feathers. Show the children how to attach the feather by wrapping string or coloured wool around the stick.

Create rain music using claves to form raindrops, maracas and shakers as the rain starts, rain sticks and drums as the rain gets heavier, etc.

The Magic Paintbrush

Julia Donaldson (Chinese folk tale)

What you need:

▶ the book or story

▶ a paintbrush, paper and an easel

▶ an old metal key

Warm up:

Pass a paintbrush around the circle. Let children come up one by one to paint one line, shape or mark onto a large piece of paper on an easel. Does a picture of anything emerge? How can they tell when the picture is finished?

Story break – Read the story that shows the paintbrush being used to paint things for poor people. Stop where the rich man or emperor finds out about the magic.

▶ **Circle of wishes** – Talk about the magic paintbrush and how everything it paints comes to life. What would the children choose to paint if they had such a brush? Pass the paintbrush around the circle again and invite children to paint their wishes. Remember the picture only comes to life when it is finished!

▶ **Please paint me a .....** – Go into role as the owner of the paintbrush. Invite the children to approach you and make requests from the story – blankets, boats, buffaloes, hats, coats, shoes, ladders, baskets, fans, etc. Try to paint the different requests! Other versions of the story see the paintbrush painting a river to water the crops, or a donkey to help a poor farmer. Invite a confident child to have a turn with the paintbrush.

Story break – Read the story up to where the owner of the magic paintbrush is thrown into prison.

▶ **Role on the wall** – Paint a picture of the rich man or emperor. Invite children to think of words to describe him. Scribe them on post-it notes and stick on the picture.

▶ **Hot seat** – Go into role as the owner of the paintbrush. Ask questions about how it feels to use the paintbrush. How will he or she escape from prison? Let the children take turns to think of ways to escape. What could the paintbrush paint to help?

Story break – Read to the end of the story. Did anybody guess correctly?

▶ **Find the key game** – Ask for a volunteer to leave the room while you hide a metal key for them to find. Ask children to use 'hot' and 'cold' or 'loud' and 'quiet' clapping to guide the child to the key's hiding place.

▶ **Physical drama** – Divide the class into three groups. Line up two groups either side of the room to be the high waves of the river. Invite the third group to pretend to be the emperor and his men in the dragon boat painted especially for him. They must try to cross the river. On a signal the waves rise up, sink the boat and drown the men.

▶ **Dragon dance** – In some versions the emperor is defeated by a painted dragon. Ask the children to form a long line and place a long piece of fabric over them. Make a dragon head from a painted cardboard box with eye holes cut out for the person at the front to hold over their head. Help the children to move up and down as they walk round the room to some traditional Chinese music.

▶ **Creative activities** – Make Chinese lanterns to decorate the room for a party to celebrate the happy ending.

The Monkey and the Jellyfish

Japanese folk tale

What you need:

▶ the book or story
▶ materials to create a jellyfish picture
▶ a glockenspiel
▶ 'Under the Sea' from Disney's Little Mermaid.

Warm up:

Move around the room in pairs. Shout out two body parts such as knee and head and the pair must join together by touching their knee to their partner's head and continue to move about. Try hand and foot or toe and tail! Let the children choose different combinations.

Story break – Read the story up to where the jellyfish is ordered by the King to go and find a monkey's liver.

▶ **Under the sea** – Use the song from the 'Little Mermaid' as background music for the children to dance and move around as different deep sea creatures under the sea. Choose two children to be the King and Queen seated on thrones. When they command, the music must stop and the other children must stand as still as statues. Those caught moving have to come and sit down by the royal couple.

▶ **Partner work** – Ask the children to work with a partner taking turns to be the monkey and the jellyfish. Start with their meeting when the jellyfish persuades the monkey to join him. Help the jellyfish to use lots of fancy praise as he talks the monkey into climbing out of the tree and onto his hard shell, e.g. 'O magnificent and marvellous monkey'. How does his speech change when they are out to sea and the jellyfish reveals his real motive?

▶ **Monkey tricks** – Ask partners to act out the encounter between the monkey and the jellyfish when the monkey pretends his liver is hanging on a tree and has to go back to find it!

▶ **Role on the wall** – Pin up a picture of the beautiful jellyfish onto the wall (see below). Help the children to write words on post-it notes to describe the jellyfish at different points of the story. Try a 'before' and 'after' session by removing the shell for the final thoughts.

▶ **Conscience alley** – Form two lines and invite children in role as the monkey and jellyfish to take turns to walk down the alley. Can they move like the different animals? Ask other children to speak out loud as though they are the animal's conscience.

▶ **Physical drama** – Ask children to find a space in the room. Can they move around like the jellyfish with lots of tentacles and a hard shell on top? On a signal such as a glissando on the glockenspiel, the jellyfish loses his shell and becomes uncontrollably wobbly! To the tune of 'Jelly on a plate' the children can sing as they wobble:

Jellyfish in the sea
Jellyfish in the sea
Wibble wobble wibble wobble
Jellyfish in the sea.

▶ **Creative activities** – Let children make a giant picture of the jellyfish to use in the role on the wall. Cut a jelly shape out of bubble wrap. Add tentacles out of strips of plastic bags. Make a removable shell from scales of shiny coloured paper and sweet wrappers.

If you have found this book useful you might also like ...

LB Making Poetry
ISBN 978-1-4081-1250-2

LB Kitchen Stuff
ISBN 978-1-4081-4048-2

LB Discovery Bottles
ISBN 978-1-9060-2971-5

LB Minibeast Hotels
ISBN 978-1-4081-4049-9

All available from
www.acblack.com/featherstone

The Little Books Club

There is always something in Little Books to help and inspire you. Packed full of lovely ideas, Little Books meet the need for exciting and practical activities that are fun to do, address the Early Learning Goals and can be followed in most settings. Everyone is a winner!

We publish 5 new Little Books a year. Little Books Club members receive each of these 5 books as soon as they are published for a reduced price. The subscription cost is £37.50 – a one off payment that buys the 5 new books for £7.50 instead of £8.99 each.

In addition to this, Little Books Club Members receive:
- Free postage and packing on anything ordered from the Featherstone catalogue
- A 15% discount voucher upon joining which can be used to buy any number of books from the Featherstone catalogue
- Members price of £7.50 on any additional Little Book purchased
- A regular, free newsletter dealing with club news, special offers and aspects of Early Years curriculum and practice
- All new Little Books on approval - return in good condition within 30 days and we'll refund the cost to your club account

Call 020 7631 5822 or email: littlebooks@bloomsbury.com for an enrolment pack. Or download an application form from our website:

www.acblack.com/featherstone

The **Little Books** series consists of:

All Through the Year

Bags, Boxes & Trays

Big Projects

Bricks and Boxes

Celebrations

Christmas

Circle Time

Clay and Malleable Materials

Clothes and Fabrics

Colour, Shape and Number

Cooking from Stories

Cooking Together

Counting

Dance

Dance, with music CD

Discovery Bottles

Dough

50

Explorations

Fine Motor Skills

Fun on a Shoestring

Games with Sounds

Growing Things

ICT

Investigations

Junk Music

Kitchen Stuff

Language Fun

Light and Shadow

Listening

Living Things

Look and Listen

Making Books and Cards

Maps and Plans

Making Poetry

Mark Making

Maths Activities

Maths from Stories

Maths Outdoors

Maths Songs and Games

Messy Play

Minibeast Hotels

Music

Nursery Rhymes

Outdoor Play

Outside in All Weathers

Parachute Play

Persona Dolls

Phonics

Playground Games

Prop Boxes for Role Play

Props for Writing

Puppet Making

Puppets in Stories

Resistant Materials

Role Play

Sand and Water

Science through Art

Scissor Skills

Sewing and Weaving

Small World Play

Sound Ideas

Special Days

Stories Fom Around The World

Storyboards

Storytelling

Seasons

Time and Money

Time and Place

Traditional Tales

Treasure Baskets

Treasureboxes

Tuff Spot Activities

Washing Lines

Writing

All available from

www.acblack.com/featherstone